SCARS OF A BROKEN HEART

ASHA SPARROW

Copyright © 2022 Asha Sparrow

All rights reserved. No part of this book may be reproduced in any form or by any electronic or mechanical means, including information storage and retrieval systems, without permission in writing from the publisher, except by reviewers, who may quote brief passages in a review.

ISBN: 978-1-955312-17-2

Printed in the United States of America

Story Corner Publishing & Consulting, Inc.

3810 Indian River Rd.

Unit 13031

Chesapeake, VA 23325

Storycornerpublishing@yahoo.com

www.StoryCornerPublishing.com

DEDICATION

I want to dedicate this book back to God because, without Him, none of this would be possible. I owe Him my life. He has saved me and kept me, and I will be forever grateful.

I also want to dedicate this book to young women out there just trying to make it and understand life. I got scars along the way trying to do it my way, but I thank God for still showing me the lessons in my scars. Ladies, remember God will always be the best source for you.

TABLE OF CONTENTS

INTRODUCTION v

CHAPTER 1
Childhood *1*

CHAPTER 2
The Love of My Life *5*

CHAPTER 3
The Trial: Death Don't Take Me Now *13*

CHAPTER 4
Love in All the Wrong Places *23*

CHAPTER 5
God Met Me in This Place *31*

CHAPTER 6
The Process of My New Walk *39*

CHAPTER 7
My New Life in God *47*

INTRODUCTION

Am I the only one who thought I would die in my trials? I thought they would take me clean out! I have struggled with depression, suicide, oppression, doubt, fear, shame, guilt, lack, loss, and low self-esteem, you name it. I have endured domestic violence, stab wounds, black eyes, being held at gunpoint, jail, heartbreaks, and so on. I know we all have a path to walk on, but mines were rough. Maybe I made some of my journey extend longer than it should have, but I am thankful I survived. I was a victim of many things, and now I can say I made it to the other side as a survivor!

This book serves as pages of hope and encouragement. I pray everyone is inspired to continue their journey after reading this book. Life gets hard at times, but with God, we can overcome anything. The testimony of my life will show you that you are not alone in the battle. We go through things and think no one else would understand because it has never been part of their life, so we tend to hind and cover it up. You will see through this story that others do understand. I am one, for example.

I desire people to read this story of my experiences and learn to make better choices than I did. I feel young people, especially women, from all walks of life can learn from my life's journey. I have kept my story in for so long, and now it is time to be released to transform others and lead them to Jesus Christ possibly. Understand that life brings different obstacles, tests, trials, and even detours, but we will walk through with victory if we don't quit.

CHAPTER 1
Childhood

They say life is a box of chocolates because you never know what hand you will be dealt. As a young girl, I saw life from many perspectives. I have seen the good, the bad, and the ugly. I would say I have had my share of all parts. That is how you paint a perfect picture when all aspects are included. I remember feeling neglected as a child but did not understand that it would impact my future. You see, my mom and dad were married, so immediately, you would think I had the perfect childhood, right? Wrong!

My mom and dad were dysfunctional at their best! I did not know if they were going or coming, and maybe because they did not know either. My mom tried her best to raise me since my dad was never around, but it just was not good enough for me. I wanted and needed more. My mom ran the streets and used drugs, so I found myself with my aunt or different babysitters. They were ok, but I wanted my mom to be there, and because she was not, I hated it! Sometimes I felt I wasn't important to my mom. I felt like I was asking for too much back then, but I guess she did not know how to supply my needs. I soon stopped asking her for anything. I accepted the way my life was going, miserable. I would see other children in my class bond with their parents and wonder why I could not have that. It was tough accepting that it was just not supposed to be part of my story. I embraced it little by little every day. It was a complicated process for me, but I managed.

My mom would be so hard on me, and I never knew why. I would pray it wasn't the whole, "I look like my dad crap." Hopefully, she didn't take her frustration out on me because of him. I still have not put my finger on why she was so hard on me, so I left it alone. My mom was verbally abusive, not affectionate, and kept her distance from me. I knew she had issues, but I accepted her and loved her anyway. Growing up, she was not the type to give hugs or even a kiss on the forehead. I could never go to her for encouraging words or even a simple compliment. I longed for that. Instead, she would tear me down! Nothing I did was ever good enough, but I continued to seek her approval until I realized that I would never get it. I wondered if this was how all moms were trained to treat their daughters until I figured she did not know how to be a mother to me. We never had a good relationship, even though that has always been a desire of mine and still is. I love my mom, but I know I need more from her. I pray every day that she changes for the better. I trust that God will make all things right in His timing.

I remember my dad trying to work it out with my mom when I was around seven years old, but they could not get through the damage already done. My dad cheated on my mom, and my mom could not see herself forgiving him. Instead, she grew angry, bitter, and mean. My mom had other boyfriends after my dad, but she was extra hard on them. She did not show that she loved them, and she would take their money. I would wonder if the men she dated were just weak or if they enjoyed the way my mom was towards them. My dad provided for us through it all, even though he was not around. I sometimes wondered if my dad had a chance to heal mentally after being shot in the head before I was born. That was one reason he lived his life all over the place. I was a little happy that my mom and dad did not work it out because I was not used to having him around. I did not want to take the time out to bond with him either. I could not find myself taking orders from someone I had hardly seen. I lost respect for him, and I was even a little upset that he could quickly leave us. I knew I wanted certain things from my mom, but I needed certain things from him as well. I got tired of waiting and did not want to be let down again if he decided to leave for a second time. I closed the door before he could even close it on me again. It broke me, but I believe I became a little stronger. All of this shaped my future relationships no matter how hard I fought. I even had to fight through school because I was not like the other kids.

I remember it wasn't until I got to college I found out I had a mental disorder called dyslexia. It was a label that hunted me. I could not understand why I was figuring it out after many years of struggling with my education. I wondered why learning was complex for me, but my classmates easily flew through assignments. I often thought of dropping out of school because of my difficulties. I did not understand the disorder back then, but I continued to fight through it. Dyslexia is a learning disorder that involves difficulty reading due to problems identifying speech sounds and learning how they relate to letters and words (decoding). It's also called a reading disability; dyslexia affects areas of the brain that process language. I was 100% sure it was because my mom did drugs while she was pregnant with me. I grew bitter, and I still blame her for it. I felt I could have been so much further in school, but I gave in to the label the system placed on me. I had low self-esteem and felt like I was not bright at all. I became the class clown acting out in class so others would not know I had a disability, as my record would show.

I struggled at birth because my mom did drugs! I was born not breathing, and my body was even blue. Everyone thought I was dead and wrote me off. God performed His first miracle in my life that day. He brought me back to life to tell the story and to set others free through my testimony. So, here I am, unfolding my life before you.

CHAPTER 2
The Love of My Life

I started young, but I was ready for love. I was a teenager that thought I knew it all. I did not realize that I would look for love in all the wrong places because of my childhood experiences. I thought this was the way of life. I remember one summer afternoon walking down the street in my neighborhood, and I heard my favorite song playing. I began to sing along with the song until I locked eyes with who was playing it. This guy was super fine, and I even think my heart skipped a beat. I walked over to him and asked him if I could have a copy of his mix CD, and the rest became history. I was so into him. He ran through my mind so much that I could not think of anything else but him. I didn't know if that was a bad thing or what, but I loved every moment of it. He was the talk of the neighborhood because all the girls had their eyes on him. I could not believe we shifted into a 'thing' so fast. It felt like a dream I did not want to wake up from just in case it was not my reality. He filled the void that had been empty for years, dating back to my childhood. I had built up love to give, and I could not contain myself. He seemed to love every minute, so much so that he gave me the same in return. I did not know if he had a void, I was filling for him, but he was comfortable around me. I also felt safe in his arms. I wanted to spend all my time with him even though I knew that was impossible.

Everything was going great between us. This guy took me on dates and was the perfect gentleman until we got into a serious relationship! Things started to change, and I could not understand why. I continued to love and be there for him, but that did not make a difference. He showed me a side of him that I would have never imagined to be him. If I did not see it with my own eyes, I would have never believed it. I told you I was young and ready for love, right? I was 14 years old, and he was 19. We thought we knew everything about love, but he had a jealous side. Love and jealousy do not mix. They are opposites. I thought it was just a phase he was going through, but that was something rooted in him. It turned our great relationship into hell!

I could not talk to another guy or look their way because I feared he would beat them up badly. I thought that maybe he would even kill someone over me. I was afraid, but he kept assuring me that he loved me because he would buy me nice things. He would make sure the expensive gifts took my mind off the questions I had in connection to his actions. It was not until his bottled-up anger was unleashed on me that I stopped accepting his gifts. When he saw he could not manipulate and control me with gifts, he became physically abusive. After he smacked me, I knew our relationship shifted into something toxic, but I stayed. I loved him and could not turn those emotions off so quickly.

He sold drugs, so he always had money to keep me quiet. He stopped giving me gifts and gave me large amounts of money. I knew I needed it, so I just took it, hoping he would change. Growing up, I saw my mom always get money from men, so I thought if guys gave me money, they loved me. I knew guys did not like to give up money, but if they did give it to someone, they were someone special to them. I just thought I was special because I was receiving money. My definition of love back then equaled money. My boyfriend would tell me he wanted to change and did not want me to leave. I believed him because I wanted it to be true. I did not want him to stop loving me, but I did not want to continue to take the physical abuse. When I thought we were good, my boyfriend would wait until my mom left the house to come over and break up stuff in her home when he was mad at me. My mom started to catch on to the pattern and was afraid to leave me alone in the house. When my mom asked my boyfriend questions about the broken items, the abuse from him escalated! I am not saying that it was my mom's fault because I knew any and everything made him lash out. My mom was trying to look out for me, and I appreciated her for that. I did not know what to do anymore. I loved him, so that kept me glued to him. I knew he loved me too, but he had issues to work out. He had trauma that he did not know how to overcome.

I remember another time my mom confronted him about marks she saw on me, then he pulled out a gun and pointed it at my head. He demanded I leave with him so that he could avoid her questioning. I was scared, so I followed his instructions. I did not want him to kill me or anyone else in the house, for that matter. I knew my mom was scared for me then, but she had to allow me to leave with him. She still followed us to make sure he did not kill me. I did not think he would kill me if I complied with his demands, but I knew he would beat me again. I was ready for the pain because I grew numb to it. I knew he thought I was telling my family about what he would do to me, and I wasn't, but I had to convince him of that. Although I was tired of our up-and-down rollercoaster, I was willing to work through it with him. I don't fully understand why. I guess it was because when we met, I had a hunger for the love and attention he gave me. It became my drug. He held it over my head like a dangling piece of meat waiting for me to bite. He gave me love in small doses to keep me returning for more. I kept returning no matter what I had to endure to get it. I felt as if I needed his love to survive! Therefore, I stopped at nothing to get it.

Another shift had occurred in our relationship, and I thought it was for the better. I found out that I was pregnant! He was so happy, but I was undecided because I was only 14. I did feel a little at ease because I figured the abuse would stop since he was excited about the baby, but it did not. He calmed down a little, though. I still walked around with bruises. After I had the baby, he returned to the usual abuse pattern. It felt like pregnancy flew by too fast. This addition changed the dynamics of my life now that I was responsible for a baby. It was no longer about me. The abuse grew to an all-time high once I thought of connecting with friends to hang out for a moment. I was just looking for a break to gather my thoughts.

One night I tried to go out, and he stabbed me in my leg. I was holding the baby in my arms and would have never thought he would do something like that. That is when I knew there was nothing ordinary about our relationship. I didn't feel loved anymore. I knew I should have been at that conclusion once he slapped me, but he stabbed me this time. That could've killed me if he hit the main artery. I was in fear all over again. It was one thing to abuse me, but to jeopardize our baby in the process was another thing. I could have dropped the baby, or even worse, he could've missed me and stabbed the baby by accident. Certain things are off-limits, and the welfare and safety of the baby are one of them. I started to rebel against him, and he would black my eyes. My mom would doctor me back to good health because I could not go to the hospital. They would ask me questions that I did not want to answer. I knew they would arrest him, but I still wanted us to work, so I covered him. I still found myself going back to him each time. I loved him even though I knew he had control over my mind. I did not know how to get it back. It was like I was a robot, and he had the controller doing whatever he wanted to me. Little did I know, he saw this behavior as a young child with his mom. His mom was in a violent relationship where the guy would beat her, and she would stay. So, he thought abusing the women he was with would make them want to stay with him. That is the love language he was exposed to; therefore, he adopted it for our relationship.

I did love him with the only love that I knew. I convinced myself to stay, thinking that one day he would change, and we would live happily ever after until I discovered he was cheating on me. He was cheating with multiple girls, and this whole time I thought I was special! I thought I was the only one. I grew angry and wanted revenge! I did not care anymore about his threats or physical abuse. I began to act out, and he could not tell me ANYTHING! He had created a monster. His abusive ways started to rub off on me, and I found myself breaking out his car windows. I destroyed anything that was of value to him. My thoughts were to take back everything I put into the relationship, but God intervened before I got lost in the madness. He got arrested on drug charges, so I was free from having to be around him.

I thanked God for stepping in because it could have been me that got arrested. Every time he wronged me, I broke out a window of his car or house. I was spared from jail each time because the cops did not catch me. At one point, I ran out of windows to break. Ha-ha. With all seriousness, though, I felt hurt that he had to go to jail because we still had a child to raise. I never imagined being a single mother. It scared me! I did not know anything about raising a baby. By this time, I was 19 years old and had to figure it out quickly. I had no role models to look up to, so I was on my own. I would visit him as much as I could so he could see the baby until I just felt that we had grown apart. After a while, it was all pointless because I lost interest in him. We had no idea when he would get out, so it seemed like a lost cause to continue to visit him. I had other things on my mind then, like how I would support a baby without money. He could not sell drugs anymore because that was what got him locked up in the first place. He was my source of income, that paid the bills and brought food. I had to think of another plan and fast. I figured the fastest way would be to get another guy to take care of my baby and me.

It was not long before I met this new guy. I found out later he knew of my baby's dad, which made me question his motives at first. He did not make a big deal about it. In fact, he accepted my baby and me. He heard around town that my baby's dad used to beat me and that he was locked up. I was shocked at how fast the word got around the neighborhood. The new guy sold drugs, too and money was no issue for him to give. He wanted to take care of the baby and me. It was too good to be true. It felt like I had hit the jackpot. I quickly closed the chapter with my baby's dad and was focused on the next man. There were moments when I reflected on the past, but I could not allow that to get in the way of my new relationship. My baby dad would even call me from time to time, and I would answer. I would put money on his books and send him care packages with things he needed. When my new boyfriend found out that I was using the money I got from him to put on my baby dad's books, he grew angry and began to put his hands on me. He would hit me just as my baby's dad did. I guess he was in fear of losing me. He thought since I stayed with my baby's dad through the abuse, that it would keep me with him too. He thought that was the only way I understood love since it wasn't anything new.

I was fed up, and I threatened to leave him, even though I did not want to go. I could not see myself living without him, but I did not want him to hit me anymore. He took excellent care of my baby and me, so I could not pass up the opportunity. The money was needed, and I did not have another source then. He thought the beatings made me stay, but it was the money. At that time, I was going through backlash with my mom. We could not see eye to eye on anything. We were always at each other's necks, and I was exhausted. I needed peace and space. I could not see myself accepting her negativity or even fussing at me any longer. I needed to move, and I needed my boyfriend to make it happen. I cried about it for too long for him not to do anything about the problem. In turn, he brought my baby and me a house! I was in love with him then! No one had ever gone that great of a length for me when I needed it the most. He even decided to move in, too, and it was okay because I figured he just wanted to take our relationship further.

Everything went well until he wanted to pick a fight. I found myself fussing and fighting with him all the time. I began to regret moving in with him because it was like I was back to living with my mom, but worse. My life was full of drama. It was good initially, and then it drastically changed. I was over having to fight all my life. I just wanted to relax and enjoy life.

I realized we had started drifting apart, so I asked him if he wanted us to separate. He assured me that he wanted to remain with me until the end. I did not think a future with him would be within reaching distance. One night I was informed by an associate of mine that he cheated on me with one of my homegirls! I could not believe it—the same pattern as my ex-boyfriend. We fuss and fight, then drift apart, and then he cheats?? I wanted to break windows out of his car for sure! With one of my homegirls, though? He could not have chosen anyone else. I guess she was the only other woman in the world besides me. I confronted him about it, and he started this big argument that led to him breaking my foot. He became irate, screaming and yelling so he could dodge my question. He realized none of that phased me, and I still wanted answers. He then forcefully shoved me, and that was all I needed to retaliate. It was 'GO' time! We started fighting, and I could only remember feeling extreme pain in my foot. I sat down to take a break, but the pain only worsened. I could not avoid the hospital then because I could barely move my foot. When adrenaline kicks in, it takes me to another dimension, and I blackout. I did not even realize at what point of the fight or how my foot got hurt. I went to the hospital, and they said my foot was broken. I was so pissed off that I did not speak to him for days.

Our relationship took a turn for the worse at that point. My boyfriend beat on me regularly then, but I stayed because he supplied my needs. He knew I had nowhere else to go, so he took advantage. I knew I needed to go because it wasn't safe to stay, but he was making many sales and bringing in a lot of money then. I felt like I would've been a fool to leave him, then someone else took my place, getting the money. I loved him, but my love for money overtook me.

CHAPTER 3
The Trial: Death Don't Take Me Now

We would fight so much that the neighbors were scared one of us would die at the other's hand. One day they decided to call the police on us as we were in the middle of an argument. When they arrived, they found drugs, guns, and money exposed. I told the police the stuff was mine so they could arrest me. I did not want him to go to jail like my baby's dad. I knew it was a crazy move, but if he had gone to prison, I would not have had any more money. Again, my goal was to protect the money because that became my focus. Money is needed for everything, and I did not want to return to living poor. I got used to the lifestyle, and I could not see myself any other way. Sure, I put my baby at the bottom of my priority list when I decided to take the blame, but I knew he could pay to get me out immediately. He had the money and then some to do it. I decided with my baby in mind. I knew I would not be locked up long and that my mom would be able to watch my baby for a little while. I had it all planned out.

I wanted the best for all of us, even if that meant me taking a fall for him. I did not want to lose him or the money. I felt obligated to do it because he cared for my baby and me without hesitation, plus I loved him. He did not convince me in any way to take the blame. In fact, he was upset that I did. I just thought that was the definition of a "rider," and I wanted to show him that I was riding for him. Why would I want to allow the boss man to go down that was paying all the bills? I would've been on the streets, and I was not having that! So, yes, I took the blame without any regrets.

I went to jail and was in a cell with ten other women. I could not believe that I was really sitting there, which was becoming part of my story. I did have to let out a few tears for me to keep on pushing. The only thing I could think of to do at that moment was to pray. I needed God to step into my mess and calm my emotions. I knew I would be out in no time, but every second felt like an hour. I never imagined experiencing feelings of the walls closing in on me. I guess the other women felt the same way because they joined me in prayer. Before I knew it, we had bonded with each other. They all were at the end of their road mentally and did not know what else to do. I was one of the few that knew God, but I did not have a deep relationship with Him. I knew He still heard my prayers because He would always show up in the least expected ways.

My boyfriend finally got through to me and let me know that he could not get me out right away. It turns out that my boyfriend could not be the one who signed for me, according to the rules they set in place. The person that signed and paid for me to get out had to have a job or records to show that they earned money. My boyfriend did not have a legal career because he sold drugs. Therefore, he could not provide the documentation needed to sign for me. He had all the money ready for me, though. Neither of us knew they would enforce that rule before I could get out of jail. We had to gather a plan fast because I was not prepared to stay in prison for too long. I told my boyfriend to ask my family if one of them could sign for me, and my uncle stepped up and did it. He could use my boyfriend's money to bail me out and show his paystubs to sign for me to get out. I was relieved that it worked. I was in jail for three weeks, and it felt like forever, but I knew God was with me there, just like he was with Joseph in the Bible days.

My lawyer began working on my case but was unsure if he would even win on my behalf. The courts wanted to charge me with delivering drugs, money laundering, and gun possession. The federal government even wanted to take over the case because of the amount of money they found in the house when they locked me up. When I went to my first hearing, I knew God was working it out for me because they dropped the gun charge and the federal government decided not to take over. At that moment, I made a promise to God that if He got me out of the mess I had created that I would serve Him with my whole heart.

My lawyer wanted me to turn in my boyfriend to get off the hook, but I could not do that because I loved him too much. I knew that if my boyfriend went to jail, he would be there for a long time because he had been there before. I trusted God would have His way with the case no matter what, so I held my peace. Soon after my first trial, my boyfriend went to jail for a different charge that had nothing to do with my case. I could not believe that I took the fall only for him to get in trouble in another situation and end up in jail. He told his workers that I would run the block in his absence. I got right to work and started moving the drugs and money around. Yes, I was a drug dealer at that point. It felt natural to me. I guess because I had been around it for some time. I had to be careful with every move I made because I was still under investigation and awaiting another trial. I ran the block for some time, and the money was rolling in just as if he were still running the block. I wanted nothing because all the bills were paid. I began to miss my boyfriend, though. I thought I could wait for him while he was in jail, but I couldn't. I needed someone to talk to, someone to bond with, someone to hold me, and someone to make me feel protected. I loved him, and I knew he loved me, but I needed him next to me. I felt like I was single again, and I grew bored. Crazy things happened when I found myself bored.

I met this guy that gave me the attention that I never knew I needed. It blew my mind, and boredom lured me into his conversations. Before I knew it, one thing led to another, and I fell for him. I gave my body to him, although I had a boyfriend in jail that allowed me to control all his money. I cheated on my boyfriend with no remorse, and at that moment, I knew our relationship would not last much longer. I still loved him, but I could feel that we had grown apart. I started attaching and catching feelings for the new guy that had my attention while my boyfriend was away. I figured since my boyfriend was still in jail, this guy would be the next new replacement. Our relationship was fun and hot. I realized I enjoyed it more because I did not need him. I wanted him. Everything was going smoothly until one night, we got into a crazy argument. I cannot even remember what it was about now. I shut down and went into stubborn mode. He tried to see if I would give in, but because I didn't, his pride made him storm away. I let him go and thought our emotions would blow over the following day until I got the phone call that he was dead!!!

The call came in at 5 am that very next morning, telling me that he got killed hours prior. I was devastated! I could not stop crying and feeling guilty. All of these "what ifs" ran through my mind. What if we had made up, and he spent the night? Would he have lived? What if we would've never argued? Would he have still died? I did not want to believe that he was gone that quickly out of my life. We were only in the "getting to know you" phase. I guess it was just not meant to be. I kept a picture to remember him, and I swiftly moved on with life to not become mentally stuck. I felt depression and anxiety creeping up on me. I had to pray hard through that traumatic experience, or I would have gone insane. Just as chance would have it, my boyfriend got out of jail after four long months. He found out that I had cheated on him. He did not act too crazy about it since the guy was dead. My boyfriend was hurt and wanted us to start over. He wanted to see if we could still be in a relationship together. I knew we were two different people at that point, but I was willing to give it a shot. We started working on our relationship, and I could see that he was serious about progressing in a new direction. I thought it would be hard for us to recover since I hurt him. Instead, he wanted to help me in every way. He even continued to help me with whatever I needed for my trial.

My trial was quickly approaching. I was nervous because I did not know what to expect. I knew God was on my side, but I did not want to go back to jail. This time they included my boyfriend in the trial somehow. My boyfriend had to get a lawyer as well to cover himself. We then found out that both lawyers wanted us to turn on each other so that one of them could get an easy win. My boyfriend and I agreed that we would not turn on each other, so the lawyers had to work the case from another angle.

I knew it was time to cash in on my promise to God. God was the only one who could cover and get me out of my mess. I quickly began to work on my relationship with God. I needed Him to show me what to do and what to say. I would seek Him daily, hoping to find the revelation I needed. I started going to church more, and I even invited my boyfriend on this one particular Sunday. I don't know why I thought to ask him, but I did. I guess it would have been nice for him to join me. He agreed, and I was shocked because he was not the type to attend church. Not that he hated God or anything, the church was just not his thing. He knew God existed, but he did not understand God's power or what He could do. I figured it was time to introduce him to God in another way because I did not go to a typical church. They knew the power of God and were not afraid of it. I knew he needed that experience to make a sound decision about the church. I wanted him to know that all churches were not the same. Some operate under the Holy Spirit, while others play "church." I don't even have time for those myself. The Sunday my boyfriend said he would attend church with me quickly arrived. I got to church, waiting for him to show up as the Pastor preached a message about life after death. Service was soon to end, and he did not show. It wasn't like him not to keep his word, so I was confused. I initially felt upset, but I figured there was always next Sunday to join me. I got home, and he told me he ran behind with time and would ensure he went next time. Next time never made it for him because days later, my boyfriend was shot dead! I was lost for words. What do I do? I thought I was next since everyone around me was meeting death. I knew the consequences of the life I was living, but I guess I never thought that they would catch up to the ones I loved or me.

The night he got shot, he called me while hanging out. He did not sound like himself and even told me he should never have gone out. He was not the club type, so I was surprised he was even there. I thought he was tired of the same scene and wanted something different. I would feel the same way when I hung out at the clubs and bars. I was bored and needed a change of scenery. One of my homies sent me a picture of them in the club. My boyfriend had this expression of terror on his face as if he had seen a ghost or knew his time was near. I thought it was strange. I asked him if he was okay, and he assured me he was fine. By that time, the alcohol had kicked in for him, and I told him I was going to bed. We hung up, and that same night he got shot in the stomach. The doctors could not understand why he did not live through it because it was not considered a major wound. The message that was preached on the Sunday he did not show up popped back into my mind. I wondered if he had shown up, would he still have been alive? Or was it just a warning for me that he would die? Was the picture another warning of his death? I had so many questions that I needed God to answer. I did not want to accept the fact that he was gone! I could not wrap my mind around it. Then again, I don't think I wanted to either.

We went through so much together that it felt like he took my heart with him when he died. I did not think it was possible to love again. It was like I had broken into many pieces, and there was no possible way to put me back together again. I was hurt and lost. I blamed myself for not appreciating him while he was living. I found myself crying out to God more than ever. I needed healing from a broken heart. I knew God heard me, but why wasn't He responding? I began to think I took too long to make good on my promise to God. I felt forsaken, as if He turned His back on me. I could not get too mad because I had plenty of opportunities to yield to God's Will for my life. I knew He loved me no matter what and did things according to what was best for me. I just had to embrace the consequences of my actions. I put myself into chaos and danger once I accepted a boyfriend who sold drugs. Drugs are a part of a fast life with quick ups and downs. It is unpredictable because you never know what will happen next. Some end up in jail for life, while others lose their lives to senseless crimes. When evil money is at the root of anything, everything is liable to fall apart. Not all money is blood money. Only when we sell our souls for the money.

Once the lawyers heard that my boyfriend died, they dropped all our charges because he died before the trial. They wanted to put the charges on him, but since he was gone, they felt there was no point in going further with the case. Yes, that was a win for me, but at the expense of my boyfriend's death. I was still grieving and did not feel like a winner at all. I prayed that God would get me out of the mess I was in, but I did not know He would do it that way. Be careful what you ask God for because He responds with His Will in mind. I believe God took my boyfriend so that I could worship Him instead of my boyfriend. I admit that I made my boyfriend my everything and put God on the back burner. I only made time for God when I needed something my boyfriend could not provide. To God, I put my boyfriend on a throne in my world. God is a jealous God, and He will not share a seat or compete with anyone. I know this, and I still messed up repeatedly. God wanted me and was not taking "no" for an answer. I made the promise, and God was waiting for me to fulfill it.

If my boyfriend were still alive, who knows where I would be? I'm sure I would not have given God all He wanted from me. I gave God some, but not all. God placed a purpose inside me that needed to be fulfilled, and I would have never yielded to God with my boyfriend around. He had that much control over my mind without even doing it on purpose. God moves people, places, and things out of the way to get our attention. They all do not necessarily die, but doors are closed, and people are cut off from access. In my case, it took death to open my eyes. Death broke me only to strengthen me for the journey ahead. I knew God was calling for me loud and clear. I could not wrap my mind around all that was happening, so I ran like crazy. I thought I could outrun God. Once I got scared, all the knowledge I knew about God went out of my head. Just know God is always everywhere; that is how powerful He is. Everything was overwhelming to me. It felt like I was on a Ferris wheel that had spun out of control. I was terrified, confused, and wished it would all STOP. I became suicidal, having thoughts of taking my own life. I thought if I were going to be next, I could help the process go faster. I sat back and evaluated my life, and I was not pleased. I became stressed and worried on top of it all. All the drugs we sold but had no savings plan in place. We had no plan in place, period. People in the market selling drugs typically do not have a plan in place because they think the money will always be there. No one plans for early deaths or lockups for life when selling drugs. I don't know why because it seems crazy now that I think about it.

I walked on the dark side because I had no one to fulfill my needs now that my boyfriend was gone. I was all over the place with this guy and that guy. I was prostituting myself for money. I never dreamed of going that low, but I had to do something quickly because jobs were not calling me back. I still needed to provide for myself and my child. Bills did not just go away. They still needed to be paid. I did not know what else to do, especially since the court proceedings were on my record. I am sure that was one of the reasons jobs were not calling me back. I was desperate, falling into a downward spiral. One night I got into the car with some guy for money, and God told me to get out of the vehicle. God said to me if I did not get out right away, I would die. That was around 2 am, and I found out that at 5 am, that same guy got shot in the head along with another person sitting in the car with him. I was thankful that it was not me, but even more emotional because it could have been me. The death angel was following me like a hawk, and I could feel it every time it came near! God was putting the brakes on me to get out of the streets, but I was stubborn. I had to learn the hard way. God marked me, and some would have mistaken this for Satan's doing. I felt death everywhere I turned. It followed me as my shadow does. God was taking away everything I loved so I could turn to Him. God wants to be our first love, as He should be. I made a promise to God, and He was looking for me to hold up my end of the deal since He held up His. God got me out of the mess I created and was waiting for me to serve Him. I took the first step by going back to church faithfully. I knew attending church was not the same as giving God my all, but I wanted more time to align myself mentally.

CHAPTER 4
Love in All the Wrong Places

    I knew I needed to take time to heal, but at this point, I did not know how. I was so used to using one guy to get over the next. I realized that was only adding layers to my pain, making it harder to turn away and break free. Even with all this in mind, I could not see myself healing while single. I tried to hold out as long as I could until this guy came about that had a crush on me for some time. I never really paid him any attention, but my mind starts to play tricks on me when I am bored and lonely. I used to work at a daycare center, which gave me joy working with kids.

    One day the guy that had a crush on me walked in to pick up his son, but I had already been bonding with the child's mother. I had no idea that he was the child's father. He started flirting with me and trying to convince me to take him up on his date request. He gave me his number to call him when I was ready. I played hard to get until I wanted to get out of the house one night, and I called him. By this time, I was laid off from my job with nothing to do. We hung out a few times and became sexually active. I soon found out I was pregnant, and everything changed! Yes, we were sexual, but I did not plan to have another baby without settling into a marriage. How did I allow it to get that far??? I had not planned on even getting into a relationship with him. We were casually dating, so I felt even crazier that I was pregnant. I barely knew him, and he knew nothing about me. I realized I did not even like him once I tried to get to know him.

I began to pray for a miscarriage because I could not see myself having his baby. I am sure the baby would have been beautiful and amazing, but I could not get over the thought of him permanently tied to my life. I started having thoughts of my previous boyfriend, that got killed. I wanted every guy to match up to him somehow, and this guy did not. I knew deep down inside that I would never find someone like my ex, but I was willing to search. Maybe I would find someone close to him. I was on a mission to find my last boyfriend in another man. Since this guy did not measure up, I did not want anything to do with him. One night of boredom should have served as a time to heal from my past. I had dug a deeper hole for myself.

The word got around town that I was pregnant by him, and his baby's mom found out. I was not hiding from her; I just did not want any problems. I have seen too many times people get into baby-mom/baby-dad drama because one moved on, but the other wanted to work it out. As much as this guy and I hung out, I was sure their relationship had been over. I did not want to deal with drama, period. It turns out I was wrong about their relationship. It was not over! The baby's mom showed up at my house one day to question me. I did not know how to respond at first because we were cool, but I felt threatened. I did not know if I wanted to curse her out or let her go on with her rant. I allowed the rant because we did have a somewhat teacher/parent relationship when I worked at the daycare. Even though I was standoffish then, she liked to talk to me but never mentioned her child's dad. I thought having those deep conversations with me was weird back then, but I allowed it because I realized she just needed someone to talk to then. Fast forward seven years later, she is at my house yelling about me being with her child's father. For some reason, I felt sympathy for her, so I lied about the whole thing so she could leave. I did not want to hurt her feelings after she revealed that she wanted a girl by him but could not give it to him.

As luck would have it, I was the one to give him a girl. I thought after I lied about everything, she would buy it and never return to my house. She came back on another occasion, so I told her the truth. She was upset and did not want anything else to do with me. I was not too bothered by that because we were never friends. We just had a teacher/parent relationship involving their son. Of course, I worked at the daycare center, so I had to talk to the parents. The baby's mom was crushed when she found out I was having the girl she always wanted. Long story short, the guy was playing us both. He ran off for months and did not want to help me with the baby. I thought he would be around because he was so excited to have a daughter with me. I was so wrong!

I started going to church more often to clear my mind and hope to get direction from God. It was just something about church that I could not get anywhere else. No matter how often I would run away, I would always find myself right back in the building. I know the church is not God, but I met with Him there a lot. I needed help, but I never sat long enough to allow God to work it out. I was so impatient with God. How many of us know that we cannot rush God? God is sovereign, so He will have all things work together according to only His plan, purpose, and on His schedule. I got tired of waiting, so I started to run the streets again. I became entangled with a lot of negativity.

It was 2009, and I was counting down the days before I gave birth to my daughter. I was running low on money, and I knew I still needed items for my baby. I did not know what to do. I could not go back to my old ways because I was pregnant. I ended up in Kmart one day browsing, and I saw two women that looked just like my dad. I thought it was strange, or maybe I was hallucinating. I followed them with my eyes around the store for a moment, wondering if I should approach them. I am sure they could feel me staring after a while. Finally, I got up enough courage to speak to them. I did not want to seem weird to them. I asked them did they know my dad, and they said, "Yes!" I was shocked and relieved at the same time. They asked me why I wanted to know. I told them they looked just like him, so I figured they must have been related. They asked me who I was, and I told them I was his daughter. They looked like they had seen a ghost and told me he was their dad too. I was speechless! I did not know if it was a good thing or a bad thing to find out that I had other siblings after all this time. I wondered if my mom knew about them. I felt my life was a mystery at this point because it seemed like I learned something new every week. I was not ready to find out I had siblings, though.

God had been telling me for some time to contact my dad's mother, but I procrastinated for a while. After I met the two women, they told my grandma about our meeting. The day before I was preparing to meet my grandma, she died! The death angel struck again. I thought the death angel was only taking the men in my life, but I see it had no limits. It takes whoever God allows it to take. I could not be mad because God told me to see her for some time, but instead, I took my time, and now she is gone. I had so many questions to ask her, but I will never see her. If only I had gone when God told me to. The two women, who I now know are my half-sisters, decided to build a relationship with me. Of course, it was one day at a time because nothing happened overnight. We would talk about our lives, catching up on the missed time. It seemed nice to have sisters who could relate to me. It felt weird at first, and then it flowed easily. To think my dad had other children out here all this time. Sometimes I wondered why my dad did not tell me I had other siblings, but then again, I probably would not have wanted to even talk to him.

It was time to put together my baby shower, even though I worried about getting all I needed for the baby. I wish I had known my sisters sooner so maybe they could have taken the baby shower job off my hands. I did not feel right asking them because of the short period we had known each other. My baby shower date had arrived before I could blink my eyes, and to my surprise, my sisters showed up! I do not expect much from people because of my past disappointments. I figured if I did not expect things, then people had no room to let me down. My sisters showed up at my baby shower and saved the day! It made me happy. Not only did they show up, but they brought so many gifts with them that I could not say thank you enough. I think they covered most of the list of things that had me worried. Look how God came through for me that fast! What a relief! I guess it is good to have sisters that care, right? I wondered how God was going to make a way out of no way for the baby supplies that I needed. He did it in an unexpected way and through strangers. The shower was beautiful. They took time to pick out each gift. I was so grateful. I could not believe all the care and love that they showed me in a short time.

After such a fantastic time, my life shifted for the worse. I fell on hard times and had nowhere to live, so my half-sisters opened their home to my oldest daughter and me. I did not trust many people, but the fact that they were willing to embrace us gave me a new perspective on people. They took care of our every need. They were hospitable and welcomed us with open arms until, one day, the enemy crept in. I was initially surprised because I was so focused on the love and help I was getting. The enemy will use whoever he can grab hold of if we are not careful. Before I could put everything together, Satan was using my half-sisters. I had let my guard down and let them in, only for them to switch up on me. Satan had entered the midst of our relationship and taken control. I was under spiritual attack and had to war in prayer! I did not want to believe it, but I knew no one was off-limits when it came to Satan. After a while, my half-sisters did not even sound like themselves. They began to do and say things that contradicted the way they had loved on me. Satan hated that I was truly happy and had real hope without a man in my life for the first time. Ephesians chapter 6 tells us that we are at war with demonic spirits, not people. I am mature enough in that area to know when spirits are at work. They were using my half-sisters to fight me for no reason. To avoid me hurting anyone, I had to go. They crossed the line, and I was not going to accept it just for a place to stay. I was pregnant, and they had the nerve to step to me as if they wanted to fight. I kept trying to figure out how it came about, but when demonic spirits are at work, they want you dead. I noticed that every time the atmosphere was turbulent, no matter where I was, I had to shift in another direction. The winds would become crazy, but I could not become shaken or bothered. I was trying to stay while it was time for me to go. God has His plans, and we have ours, but God's plans will always prevail. God allowed me to meet them and for them to bless me, but it was time to go.

Seasons changed quickly, but I had to be okay with that. I was on my way to where ever God wanted me to be next. My half-sisters grew to hate me, but I knew it was the push I needed to complete the transition. I am too friendly sometimes, so I tend to linger in places or stay with people I should not. Hence, the story of my life. I have a distant relationship with my half-sisters now. I like to look at it as a work in progress. I do not like the fact that I always check on them or we do not speak. I know God is training me to be the bigger person, but sometimes it hurts. Sometimes I do not want to be the bigger person! I want to please God with my life, so why not start here? I feel that since we are family, things should be different. I thought they would at least want to check on me too. Guess it doesn't matter to them anymore. I must constantly remind myself that none of this is about me. It is more significant than me. I know I did nothing wrong for them to push me away, so I will continue to check in on them and move on. I pray they will find it in their hearts to move past the situation, so our relationship can be restored one day. Until then, I will pray for my half-sisters and wait for God to move.

CHAPTER 5
God Met Me in This Place

I began to seek God even more. I needed answers in life. I wanted to know what my purpose was. I believed there had to be more to life for me. I did not want to accept what I had seen so far. I could feel that there was more to life, but I did not know what. I decided to seek the one who created all of this and us to get the answers I had been seeking. It was driving me crazy. I just had to know. I would pray morning, noon, and night. I was desperate to know what my next chapter held. I felt incomplete and thought that the answers would fill my void.

I was a pregnant single mom, and life was getting harder. I knew when I gave birth to my second daughter, life would try and chew me up! I needed to be prepared, but the only way I could do that was to seek God for guidance. Sometimes, I felt nervous and alone, but I knew I could count on God. I was grateful to know that God was always near without a shadow of a doubt. I just had to allow Him access to come in and work. I gave birth to another beautiful baby. God sustained me and provided for me every step of the way.

One morning I went into prayer as usual, and God told me He was calling me higher. I scratched my head with that one because I felt as if I was barely getting by each day. He wanted me to accept the calling of "Minister" on my life. I almost ran away when I heard that part. I was overwhelmed with emotions and thoughts. Indeed, I thought God was talking about that for the far future, but it was a "right now" word. I was shocked and honored that He would even want to choose me, but He did. Tears flowed from my eyes uncontrollably. He also told me that the ministry I was a member of did not want to ordain me because they did not think I was a good fit. God assured me that He would force the ministry to yield to His Will to ordain me anyway. I did not want any trouble or drama from the church, but I had to obey what God wanted me to do. I gave God an honest YES, and He did the rest.

The ministry ordained me as Minister, and I felt a shift in my life. I started bringing people to church left and right. I was passionate about seeing God's people saved, healed, and delivered. I knew what freedom felt like, and I just wanted everyone to get a chance to experience it for themselves. That went on for some time until I hit another wall in my life. The enemy was after me like never before. He did not want to see people free, and he wanted me stuck going in circles. He knew if he could distract me, the flow of people attending church would slow down or even stop. I fought hard, but he succeeded once he preoccupied me with my problems. It was a cycle I was stuck going round and round in. I would hit a significant problem, fall into depression, then sin to take my mind off the pain. I would try to drink it away, smoke it out, or sex it away. Either way, I had to do something strange to take my mind off my problems. I became so indulged in depression and distracted by the issues that I walked away from the church. This time was different because I was held to a higher standard, being as though I was a ministry leader. I thought I was a little more grounded in my walk of salvation, but that crafty enemy made enough noise to make me take my eyes off God. I felt like I had let God down. He invested so much in me, yet I am back in sin after saying I was done.

When I walked away from the church, everyone I led there walked away too. When I found that out, I felt so guilty! They blamed me for their downfall, but moreover, I blamed myself for them. I had blood on my hands because I was supposed to be a role model of Jesus Christ. After a while, I laid down the calling on my life as Minister and roamed wild! I did not realize how deep I was going into darkness and walking further away from God. Bad enough, I was consumed with my problems, but I was overwhelmed with the guilt I felt when the ones connected to me fell away from God. The only thing that helped me through the guilt and shame was to ask God to forgive me and the revelation that everyone must work out their self-salvation. I pointed them to Christ with the seed or the water, which was my job, and God had to do the rest. I cannot be God because I would never measure up. Only He can change people. I can barely change my actions. I need help from the Holy Spirit daily! I know the walk of Salvation is challenging but doable if we allow the Holy Spirit to work in and through us. The great Apostle Paul in the Bible understood this best when he said, "Follow me as I follow Christ." Apostle Paul knew if he was not leading the people to Christ, he was leading them away to be caught by Satan in the slaughterhouse. I know the ones connected to me that walked away from church did not have a connection with God, and that is very important to grow spiritually. They were trying to have a relationship with God through me, and God does not want that. He desires a one-on-one relationship with us all. I am working my relationship out with Him one day at a time. I know I must do better with looking past distractions and not getting caught up. I want to be better every day, so I will no longer take the blame for someone else's shortcomings. God sees all and knows all.

I also know gifts and callings come without repentance, meaning if God wanted to use me, He would, despite me walking away and laying down my calling, but my heart was not in it. My heart was contaminated, and God wanted no part of that. Just because God uses us does not mean we are going to heaven. Our hearts must be pure, our hands must be clean, and we must operate in the spirit of God. Every day I tried my best to work myself back to God. Many of us say God leaves us in our dark times, but truth be told, we leave Him thinking we can supply a result better or faster. I walked away from God, and it was time for me to get back. I did not want the death angel to take me out. I had kids to look after.

God began to show me miracles right before my own eyes. I could not make this stuff up even if I wanted to! I know God is real without a shadow of a doubt. I just had to line back up. God allowed me to anoint a baby's eyes, and he could see without help from doctors. God used me to anoint a lawyer's hand and a courtroom door, so my cousin's murder charges could be dropped. God performed a miracle before so many that doubted my cousin had a chance to beat the charges. I could never forget when God had all the charges dropped from my court case, so I know He is a miracle worker. God even allowed me to give His word to a prostitute as I walked by her. God told me to let her know that she could not get into the car that pulled up for her at that moment. He told me to tell her that if she got in the car, that would be her last day on earth. I was shocked when God revealed that to me, but even more shocked that I had to deliver those words to her. I remember when I would get into different men's cars for money! I am so glad that God protected me through it all, so I had to tell her, nervous and all. I remember walking up to her as she opened the car door, and I asked her to come with me. She told me she needed money for her medicine, so she had to get in the car. I thanked God that I had some cash on me, so I could walk her to the store to pay for her medicine. She did not get into the car and lived another day. I even remember smoking weed one day, and God began to speak to me. Of all the times He could have spoken, He spoke while I was getting high. God told me if I smoked weed again, my mom would die. The fear of God flooded my whole body to the point that I was not even high anymore. I consider this a miracle, too, because God did not have to warn me. He could have just taken my mom without a word and forced me to get myself together, or I would have been next. The fact that God still showed me love and kindness even while I had a blunt in my hand, I am forever grateful! God gave me grace beyond grace. I could never earn it, nor did I deserve it. God told me to stop smoking weed, so I could have a sober mind to stand in the gap for my mom in prayer. God was using me, and I was unsure why because I was young and running wild.

I finally got back to church, and I felt relieved about it. The church is where I could unwind and be at peace to hear God clearer. I feel like once I sit down, I understand life a little bit better while I am there. At one service, a woman approached me and began to encourage me. I thought it was strange because she did not know me, but I knew we knew a person in common. It was God, and He knows me very well. He began to reveal things about me to her. As she opened her mouth to confirm what God was telling her, I was at ease with her because it was all true. The woman said that God was calling me higher and wanted me to walk into the office of a Pastor. I almost fell to the floor, and I just knew she had misheard that! All I could think about was that He called me to Minister, and I could not even get that right. So why would He want me to go higher? I did not understand. In the world, there is a saying, "If it doesn't apply, let it fly." Therefore, I surely let that part fly!

I was the same one who first encountered God in a bathroom. The place where people say God does not go because it is dirty and smelly. I can tell you firsthand that those people that say that are speaking a lie. They put limits on God that He never set in place.

God's Word tells us about the parable of the shepherd leaving the ninety-nine sheep to find the one lost sheep. Jesus lets us know that He is The Great Shepard, and He too will leave the ninety-nine to find that one that is lost. It did not say all places except the bathroom or this list of places. No, Jesus will go wherever He has to go to get whoever is lost. I was indeed lost and ended up in a bathroom one night after partying so hard. I remember sitting there trying to gather myself after smoking weed and drinking heavily. I lived fearlessly with no regard for anything. I did what I wanted and when I wanted to do it. This night was different because I was trying to figure out how to make it home safely without getting into a car accident. All while nodding off in the bathroom as the alcohol took over, God spoke to me for the first time! It scared me so bad that I began to sober up immediately. I thought I was going crazy because I knew I was the only one in the bathroom. God met me there that night, and I am thankful for it because I am today to tell the story. I would have survived getting home that night without Him. He loves me more than I will ever know. Just know He loves you too. If you are dealing with something and feel alone, He is with you always. Just let Him in to meet the need. "Ask, and it will be given to you; seek and you will find; knock and the door will be opened to you." Matthew 7:7 NIV.

    I owe my life to God because it could have been gone so many times, but He spared me. God has been so many things to me. God is and will always be my best friend. I used to have a couple of best friends, but I had to move them to other categories, such as associate. God showed me the true meaning of friendship. He kept my secrets and never told anyone. I did not have to worry about my business being published and everybody laughing at me. I could tell God anything, and He never made me feel less than others. Yes, He told me when I was wrong, but He did it all in love and kindness. To love is to be kind, and He showed me that daily. God was different, and nobody could ever compare to Him. God is my protector. He was there for me when my first baby's dad shot at me, stabbed me, and even when I went through beating after beating. God did not allow me to die. He always rescued me when He knew I was at my maximum pain tolerance. God was there. He held back a lot of things that could have happened. Things could have been a lot worse, but God covered me even in my disobedience. He is also ABBA (Father) to me. God stepped in when my biological father left me. God taught me and trained me through it all, and He still does.

God is my lawyer, pleading the case on my behalf. He fought for me and wanted me to win. I remember I got into trouble years ago, and the lawyer I hired doubted he would even win the case on my behalf. God went to war for me then and still does. God is my doctor. When the doctors told me there was a possibility I had cervical cancer, God was there and changed the doctor's report. I could praise Him all over again just off that alone! I know people who died from that, but God covered me from it. God is also my way-maker. He has made ways out of no way. When I thought I would not make it, God showed up and turned the whole situation around for my good. The situations that were impossible for me to do anything in them, God revealed that with Him, all things are possible. The crazy part is that I am still learning to allow Him to be a way-maker in my life because I am used to being in control. I sometimes revert to being afraid, anxious, doubtful, and impatient when I am not in control. To experience God as a way-maker, we must relinquish control over to Him and trust that He will make a way. God is everything to me. I could go on and on with the many titles that He wears in my life, but we would be here all day. Know that God can be anything you need Him to be in your life, too, according to His Will for your life.

Although I walked away from the church, I found myself doing ministry anyway. God has a funny way of getting purpose out of us. God revealed to me that He placed a ministry within me and that I needed to birth it out. He gave me the name of the ministry, and it is "God's Hands and Feet Ministry." God gave me this name to show people He is still alive. Through the ministry He brought forward through me, He showed His people His hands and feet. The hands of God are always ready to extend love and kindness to us. His feet represent Him standing close, interceding on our behalf, and teaching us His ways. He walked first so that we shall follow His lead. God had me going out to the street corners praying for the people. I was teaching the Word of God and giving out food, water, and Bibles. I did this ministry for about nine months. My heart is to give back to God's people and for God to use that for His glory. I extended myself however I could and still do.

I enjoyed doing ministry, but I took a break from it all because of my selfish reasons. I still desire worldly things or things opposite of God from time to time, like partying and hanging out with people that means me no good. God has a purpose for me and I have to follow His rules so I can complete that mission. I can not allow people, places, and things continually get in the way. Sometimes it's hard doing things God's way when you have so many doing the opposite and making it look fun or you are used to doing something that makes you feel good then God tell you to stop. I knew I must give God my all and be on fire for Him to please Him. I did not want to play with God or the assignments He gave me to do, so I decided to put down the ministry. I chose to satisfy my flesh with my desires instead of God's. I knew there was a purification and deliverance process that I had to go through, and I was at peace with that. I was ready to allow God to help me because I could not do it myself. I tried too many times on my own and failed. I trusted God with my life because He was the one who gave it to me in the first place. The walk with God is no easy task, but He is the difference between possible and impossible. With God, all things are possible and I will not give Him up.

CHAPTER 6
The Process of My New Walk

I knew I needed deliverance from fleshly desires because when the struggle came upon me, it took over! Therefore, I knew that was a job that only God could do. I did not want to be a hypocrite like leaders I have seen before, so I just laid it all down to do what I wanted. I did plan on going back out to the streets to minister, but it would be whenever God led me. I wanted to be in right standing with God and completely obedient to Him. I know I sometimes mess up, but I am just thankful that He forgives and extends mercy and grace to me. God gives chances, and I am a living witness that can testify to that.

Looking back over my life, I began to see patterns and cycles, none of which were good. I began to ask God why and it was because of my choices. It was time for me to get myself together and allow God to take over. I knew God wanted to deliver me from my ways, but I had to be open to it. It seemed like every time I was ready for God to step fully into my life, I always became distracted. Either person, place, or thing grabbed my attention. I know the devil is very crafty, but I have allowed him in for too long. He has contaminated parts of my life, and I could not have him taking over. I knew God was waiting on me to surrender, but fear sometimes made me procrastinate. I guess the saying is true, "when you are sick and tired of being sick and tired, you make a move quickly." It took me a while to reach that point. I was tired of the negative cycles but needed a push. My thought process was to surrender to God and not return to my old ways once I was ready. So, I enjoyed myself a bit longer to ensure I was done.

The chapters in my life changed once again, and I met this new guy. Of course, I am sure you all have heard this story before. Ha-ha. He was sugar, spice, and everything nice. He sold me a dream that I just knew would come to reality. We dated for some time until things started to change, and those cycles reappeared in my life. When we do not allow God to be the head of our life, anything is liable to happen. Nothing works out in life without God because He already has a set plan for us. You see, I thought I was having fun outside of God, but really, I was in darkness. Darkness is death because you do not know where you are. It's like a lost place or a maze you will never get out of unless God leads you. In the dark place, you lose time, sleep, resources, energy, sanity, etc. It's not just a lost place; it's a place of loss. Grief, pain, and suffering dwell in the dark place as well. When I realized the lost place was taking me deeper, I needed a savior all over again! I guess this was my place of sick and tired of being sick and tired. I quickly surrendered because I knew death was also waiting in the darkness. I had too much I wanted to accomplish, so I had to act fast without procrastination. I was over the cycles of people, places, and things. God stepped in, and I could feel the relief. The devil did not want me to choose God as my head because he wanted me to stay in darkness with him. I took a stand and said enough was enough. All the fun I thought I was having only planted evil seeds to set me back. I am so glad that God gives us grace and mercy. He loves us enough to give us things we do not even deserve. I am grateful for the chance to serve such a mighty King, Master, and Creator.

God began dealing with me about a prophecy a lady released to me a while back. She said God was calling me higher in Him. I was not trying to hear about going higher when I barely made it where I was. I know the higher you go spiritually, there will be more warfare. The devil was mad and on my trail! Therefore, I knew he was arranging traps for me. I did not want to fall again or let God down after I gave Him my word. I realize many things in life are a test to see where we are mentally, emotionally, spiritually, and physically. God was calling me to the office of Pastor. I was hesitant because as soon as I accepted the office of Minister, all hell broke out in my life, and I left the church. I felt better, allowing the world to help me cope back then. I did not want any repeats. The devil is a crafty creature, even though I try my hardest not to be fooled by him. I gave God a YES, so I had to follow through with my word. I was nervous and knew only God could keep me through the journey.

When God wants a thing, it will happen even if we try to resist or run. We can take detours or even waste time, but God will ultimately get what He wants. I knew I had to answer the calling of Pastor because although I did not want the warfare, the warfare found me! When you are disobedient, warfare has no standards or boundaries. It will let loose on you, and you will not even know what hit you. Now, that is not to say that God won't get you worse because you do not want to mess with Him. I need God's protection in all things, especially climbing to another level in the spiritual realm. I decided to be obedient and give God all of me. That required me to lay down the ways I adopted from the world and follow His son Jesus. They say to know better is to do better. I sometimes struggle with doing better, but I want to please God. I had to be committed.

I changed ministries and sat for a while. I had no problem with it. I enjoyed the time we all gathered. One day the ministry leader announced she was putting together an installment service, and she included me. I was floored and caught off guard. She began to prepare for the date, and I became so nervous that I broke into a sweat just thinking about it! I knew it was God telling me it was my time. I thought I still had more time to get myself together, but apparently, I did not. It was now or never. I did not want God to come after me, so I surrendered. I gave God another YES and continued with the process. When you give God a real YES from your heart, God does perform miracles in your life. He gives you favor that does not even compare to all the money in the world. He gives blessings that you could have never dreamed. I know God is there for me, so I must stay aligned with His plans and be about His business.

I love God, don't get me wrong. At times I find myself choosing other things over Him when I am afraid. When I do that, it tells God that I am not 100% for Him. It saddens my heart when I think about it because He has been better than good to me. God does not want us halfway in. He wants all or nothing, and this I know. I try my hardest to work on this daily because He loves me, and I love Him. This new YES I gave God was different, and I could feel it. Before I knew it, hell broke out everywhere I turned yet again. Everything and everyone began to get on my nerves! I knew that it was a test to see if I would turn back to my old ways. I could not allow stress to break me that easily again. I should have seen it coming. I had to take one day at a time consistently. My prayer life even had to elevate. If I made one wrong move, the devil would be waiting to take me out. I could not let him win, so I continued to stay focused.

I had to undergo a training process with the ministry that would install me as a Pastor. They took me through the wringer! I was questioned left and right by one leader that did not believe in me. She did not honor that God called me to Pastor. I constantly had to prove myself as if she was God, and I had to bow to her every request! I felt if she did not release me, I would not have been able to go forward within ministry. I knew God had already called and chosen me, so I was not worried about her opinions. I was just annoyed with the whole process! I am glad I am not weak-minded or naïve to who God is in my life. I knew God called me for a time such as this, no if people believed in me or not. I was ready because God said so! I continued through the process, hoping God would pull me out. I had to devote myself to prayer each day fully, or I do not think I would have made it to the installment service without telling people off. I was mishandled and looked down upon because they thought little of me. It was a mental and emotional fight to walk in the calling God placed on my life, let alone get a piece of paper signed by them. When you have people trying to stand in the way of a move of God because they don't want to line up or keep you stuck in a place they think you should be, it makes everything harder.

Don't get me wrong; I gave God my YES. Therefore, I was willing 100%. Otherwise, I would have never chosen this path for myself. So, when others tried to block the plans of God for my life, it made me upset and rethink being a part of that church. All this made me look back to when I was to be installed as a Minister. They did not believe in me or think that I was ready either. I wondered how I joined another ministry where God wanted to elevate me again, and the same thing was happening. I did not understand. I understood Jesus dealt with people not receiving him and denying the fact that he was the son of God. I thought it would be a little better going through the process because they seemed to like me. I even thought we were friends. But I guess when God's Will goes into effect, some people fall off, and others show they never liked you. Again, I did not choose this path for myself, but I did give God all of me to do whatever He wanted. Therefore, I walk boldly excepting the call of Pastor on my life.

After many ups and downs, the training process was over, and the installment day had finally arrived. I thought the day would never come and there were even talks about canceling the service because so many things were going on behind the scenes of the ministry. Once I saw that, I thought God would release me from the church! I wanted to throw my hands up and be done with it all, but God told me to stay and pray about it all. I had to pray for myself, everyone else installed that day, and the ministry. They went forward with the service, and I became Pastor. I went through a lot, but I made it to the other side. Months later, a complete turnaround happened in the ministry. I thank God for the opportunity to pray to Him, and He moves according to His Will. I am honored to serve a God that is present everywhere at one time and knows all from beginning to end. He knew all that would happen in the ministry. He knew what would happen involving the installment service, so He covered me from the tricks and plans of the enemy. I accepted my certification and continued to do the work as a Pastor. It was a different feeling.

I felt another shift that was even greater than what I had ever experienced in my life. The change was so drastic that the things from my past started to resurface. I knew Satan had a plan and traps set for me. He did not want me to be free; instead, he wanted me to go backward. I knew I could not go back because nothing was there for me. So many things began to happen that what was behind me got my attention. I looked back and got hypnotized. Problems occurred that I was not prepared to deal with at that moment. I did not know how to cope with all the warfare that was going on. I figured if I ran, the warfare would stop. So, I ran away as fast as I could. I ran so fast that I fell into the arms of another man! I thought he could comfort and be there for me through the storm. Why did I think someone else would understand the assignment God placed on my life??? I barely understood at times. We began to spend a lot of time together until one devastating day I discovered I was pregnant again! Yes, you heard what I said. I was pregnant. Of course, I did not sign up for that, nor did I think it would even be possible. I knew if I kept playing Russian roulette, I would get caught. I did not believe it would happen with this guy while hell was breaking out in my life again. I thought I was safe to keep having fun. I was even at the point of leaving the guy alone because I knew he was not someone long-term. Now pregnant??? How would I walk away then?

I was so hurt because I wanted to be married before I had another child. I wanted to do the right thing before God. Plus, children should be raised in a two-parent household so they can get everything they need. I wanted a husband but could not wait on God to reveal Him to me. I grew impatient and chose relationships for myself. I would get hurt or realize I was wasting my time, then feel regret. I had to put an end to the cycle in my life. I needed God to step in and make the change. I had no self-control and had to pull it together. I was having another baby by another man that I knew was not the one for me. He was not the one that would make me happy, and I messed up by playing around with him. I was depressed and would cry every day. I was tormented with regret for the whole pregnancy.

I asked God why I had to keep getting pregnant by random guys even though I thought I was being careful. Why did I only attract guys that did not want to do right by me? Why were these the cycles of my life? God revealed this baby was to slow me down because I was moving too fast. God reminded me that His children are blessings no matter how I feel. I made a mistake, and it was time to pay the consequence. All I could think about was not wanting to have her every day. I considered abortion but was too scared of God to follow through. God let me know that my baby would be great in Him and that she was called to the nations. The enemy heard that and tried to kill her in my womb. She pulled through because God's hand was on her. When God has a purpose for your life, He has the final say regarding what will happen with your life. It was not her time to go. That was a wake-up call for me, and I knew it was time to get back to church. In the church is where I could get spiritually still enough to hear God crystal clear. I had to stop running and playing around because I was carrying God's purpose, my baby. Although the life I thought I wanted to live seemed amazing, it was just a watered-down version of all God had for me. I had to trust God with all my heart and keep moving forward!

CHAPTER 7
My New Life in God

God requested me to go on a 21-day fast. Christians often fast to seek guidance from God. The word "fast" means to abstain from food or drink (except water) for a certain period. I thought twenty-one days was a long time to fast, but with God, all things are possible. When I started the fast, God began to show me who He was in my life all over again. This time on a greater level. God revealed He wanted all of me and not just a percentage anymore. God told me He could and would provide for my every need. The Lord wanted my trust. Therefore, He closed the door on others, preventing them from helping me.

God wanted me to see Him as the only provider. I recommitted myself and allowed the Holy Spirit to show me how to live life. My mind changed, and my perspective was focused on doing the Will of God. It was all I could think of each day. I wanted to do ministry as God would have it, but I needed to be fully delivered from my past. I still suffered from the passing of my boyfriend and the heartbreaks of everyone who let me down. I had so many questions concerning life. I wondered why I attracted people who were abusive in relationships. I stayed with them, hoping they would change for the better. I thought I could fix people once I saw that they were damaged. I have always encountered people who needed help mentally, emotionally, and spiritually. It was not until I realized that the only one who could change people was God that I had more peace. If I had allowed God to lead me to the man He created for me, I would not have experienced so much heartbreak. I know now that God repairs all who allow Him. Therefore, I am on a journey of elevating my trust and faith in God. He has never let me down, and I'm confident He will continue to be there for me.

God is the way to eternal life and truth. It is essential to go deep in our relationship with Him for the answers we desire because He knows everything. Going deeper into God means more prayer, fasting, reading, and studying His Word throughout the Bible. There is safety with Him. He is everything we need and even things we do not know we need. Scripture compares Him to water because our bodies cannot survive without it. It is vital for us. I pray we all get to meet Jesus to obtain salvation. Salvation is to accept Jesus as Lord over your life so He can take control. When Jesus takes control, one is saved and has the opportunity to enter Heaven. Eternal life awaits us in Heaven.

Without God, we are nothing, and I learned that the hard way. I now allow His Holy Spirit to guide me when I do not know what to do. My relationship with God is personal and sacred because I realize I need Him daily. I have come to love God more than anything. I cannot put others before Him anymore. It had almost cost me my life. Even the people and things I did lose cost too much. It took me a long time to get to this point, but I cherish God. When people walked out of my life, God was there through it all. When I had nothing, God was still there. When they lied on me and turned their backs on me, God was there. When they used and abused me, God was still there, waiting for me to accept Him. Even when I put other people before Him, God still patiently waited for me. God never left me, and I am forever grateful! I mean it with my whole heart when I say I love God.

Colossians 3:23-24 NIV

Whatever you do, work at it with all your heart, as working for the Lord, not for human masters, since you know that you will receive an inheritance from the Lord as a reward. It is the Lord Christ you are serving.

Everything in this world, including materialistic things, is all vanity and will pass away at some point. When we stand before God during judgment, God will ask us to give an account of all the things that we were supposed to do, did do, wanted to do, and the things we should have done. We worry about so many things, none of which are the assignments God laid out for us. When we do not walk in God's purpose for our lives, we are in error. No paycheck, person, or place is worth being out of alignment with God. We will have to give an account for that, too, on judgment day. We must follow Jesus no matter what.

I am at a place in my life where I tell God every day to take over. I understand it's not my will but His Will that needs to be done in my life and my children's life. I am reminded of the scripture, Joshua 24:15 ESV "And if it is evil in your eyes to serve the Lord, choose this day whom you will serve, whether the gods your fathers served in the region beyond the River, or the gods of the Amorites in whose land you dwell. But as for me and my house, we will serve the Lord."

I must constantly choose to serve God even when it does not look favorable. The enemy fights for me to serve him every moment, but I can't look back like Lot's wife because I will become the pillar of salt. I do not want to be useless to God any longer. I want to fulfill my purpose and please God. There are only two entities in life to serve. Either we choose Satan or God because there is no in-between. Every day I must beat my flesh under subjection so I do not fall into Satan's traps of temptation. I cry out to God regularly to take the thorn of partying, drinking, and smoking out of my side so I can live my best life. God let me know that His grace was sufficient for me and that I had to allow Him to be God in my life.

In conclusion, God can find you no matter how deep you are in darkness. Even if you ran as fast as possible, God would still be there. God is our best option. He is our only option. No matter what you are going through, nothing is too hard for God because everything is possible with Him. He will work everything out for our good because the battle is not ours but His. We have to love Him. Don't give up!

God loves us so much that He gave up His only son for us. If God located me and brought me back into His light, He can do the same for you! Jesus Christ left the ninety-nine to find "the one" that got away. He did not care how long it took to find "the one" or what He had to go through to locate "the one." Jesus loves us that much. I was "the one" a few times in my life. I am grateful that Jesus would come after me again and again. If you are "the one," know it's only due time that Jesus will also find you. We are children of The King, and He would stop at nothing to show us His love. When man changes his mind about us, God will be there the same yesterday, today, and forever more. God saved me because He is just that good. God is the creator of all things, including me. I am grateful to be alive, even if life is hard sometimes. I do not have to go through it alone but with God, which makes all the difference. No matter how many scars you have, there is beauty behind it all. Never forget to value yourself because God does.

My life scripture:

Psalm 139 NIV

You have searched me, Lord,
and you know me.
You know when I sit and when I rise;
you perceive my thoughts from afar.

You discern my going out and my lying down;
you are familiar with all my ways.
Before a word is on my tongue
you, Lord, know it completely.
You hem me in behind and before,
and you lay your hand upon me.
Such knowledge is too wonderful for me,
too lofty for me to attain.

Where can I go from your Spirit?
Where can I flee from your presence?
If I go up to the heavens, you are there;
if I make my bed in the depths, you are there.

If I rise on the wings of the dawn,
if I settle on the far side of the sea,
even there your hand will guide me,
your right hand will hold me fast.
If I say, "Surely the darkness will hide me
and the light become night around me,"
even the darkness will not be dark to you;
the night will shine like the day,
for darkness is as light to you.

For you created my inmost being;
you knit me together in my mother's womb.
I praise you because I am fearfully and wonderfully made;

your works are wonderful,
I know that full well.
My frame was not hidden from you
when I was made in the secret place,
when I was woven together in the depths of the earth.
Your eyes saw my unformed body;

all the days ordained for me were written in your book
before one of them came to be.
How precious to me are your thoughts,[a] God!
How vast is the sum of them!
Were I to count them,
they would outnumber the grains of sand—
when I awake, I am still with you.

If only you, God, would slay the wicked!
Away from me, you who are bloodthirsty!
They speak of you with evil intent;
your adversaries misuse your name.

Do I not hate those who hate you, Lord,
and abhor those who are in rebellion against you?
I have nothing but hatred for them;
I count them my enemies.
Search me, God, and know my heart;
test me and know my anxious thoughts.
See if there is any offensive way in me,
and lead me in the way everlasting.

The scripture below has gotten me through so much in my life. God has continually brought me out of the dark valleys because His Word said He would. I will be forever grateful that He didn't leave me there to die. I wanted to share the scripture with you all as encouragement. If He did it for me, surely He wants to do it for you.

Psalm 23 NIV

A psalm of David.

The Lord is my shepherd, I lack nothing.
He makes me lie down in green pastures,
he leads me beside quiet waters,
he refreshes my soul.

He guides me along the right paths
for his name's sake.
Even though I walk
through the darkest valley,
I will fear no evil,
for you are with me;
your rod and your staff,
they comfort me.

You prepare a table before me
in the presence of my enemies.
You anoint my head with oil;
my cup overflows.
Surely your goodness and love will follow me
all the days of my life,
and I will dwell in the house of the Lord
forever.

When life throws you lemons, remember to smile and make lemonade because:

Philippians 4:13 NIV

I can do all this through him who gives me strength.

Keep going, and do not give up!

www.ingramcontent.com/pod-product-compliance
Lightning Source LLC
LaVergne TN
LVHW020439080526
838202LV00055B/5261